When I Grow Up

Written by Joellyn Cicciarelli

Grown-ups keep asking me,
"What do you want to be?"

Sara says she wants to be
an astronaut.
She likes to go places.

Maybe I'll be an astronaut, too.
I could go to the moon,
find a new star,
or maybe even meet an alien.

But maybe not.

Tim says he wants to be a chef.
He likes food.

Maybe I'll be a chef, too.
I could make peanut butter
sandwiches, lots of cookies, or
maybe a pizza birthday cake.

But maybe not.

Sue, Kim, and Cara say they
want to be doctors.
They like helping people.

Maybe I'll be a doctor, too.
I could listen to heartbeats,
fix broken arms, and maybe
give shots that never, ever hurt.

But maybe not.

Kevin says he wants to be
a zoologist.
He likes animals.

Maybe I'll be a zoologist, too.
I'll find out how birds fly,
where elephants live, and
everything there is to know
about turtles.

But maybe not.

Nicky says she wants to be
a builder.
She likes to make things.

Maybe I'll be a builder, too.

I'll build a brand-new house
for my family and a really tall
building for the whole world
to see.

But maybe not.

Janet says she wants to be President.
She likes being an American.

Maybe I'll be President, too.
I could make laws that keep people safe and ride in parades on the 4th of July.

But maybe not.

Selma says she wants to be
an Olympic swimmer.
She likes sports.

Maybe I'll be an Olympic
swimmer, too.
I could win lots of medals
and stand very proud when they
play the "Star-Spangled Banner."

But maybe not.

Oh, what will I be when I grow up?

I guess I'll just have to wait and see.